FULL CIRCLE

Llew at Llyn y Fan Fawr.

Full Circle

The Life
of
Llew E. Morgan

Carole Morgan Hopkin

GOMER

First impression—April 1997

ISBN 1 85902 586 2

© Carole Morgan Hopkin

Printed at
Gomer Press, Llandysul, Ceredigion

This Book
is Dedicated
to my sister,
Wendy.

ACKNOWLEDGEMENTS

Grateful acknowledgement is made to the following for their help: William H. Booth A.M.P.A., L.B.I.P.P.; Dic Davies; Ruby Kingston Gibbs; Josef Herman O.B.E., R.A.; John Hines; Elizabeth Hopkin (for copyright permission); 'Skip' Morgan O.B.E.; William B. Richards PhC.; M.R. Pharm. S.

FOREWORD

The world was held in a magic box cradled in my grandfather's arms.

The magician, Llewelyn Morgan, was lord of the Swansea valley, and our Kingdom spread wide at both ends, over the Gower peninsula to the south, and here, behind Ystradgynlais, ranging past the Brecon Beacons to our wildlife paradise of Rhandir-mwyn, places recalling Merlin and the Mabinogi.

Photography was a trick which let you hold an experience in your hands—a new-born lamb on shaky limbs, a peregrine falcon in full-flight, the sun dipping behind storm clouds, me as a Gower mermaid; me here holding me there in the picture.

Before I could wield a brush I watched, entranced, as grandfather formed a strawberry on an empty page, a luscious fruit ripe for eating, with a bead of dew caught in its pitted rosiness. Out of a paintbox he conjured flowers, the glint in a rabbit's eye, hills and vales, clouds and waves.

On wild nights, as storms raged on the conservatory roof, and Gran's geraniums trembled at the onslaught, we would beg to see the German's thumb. Grandfather refused, though only to make us plead harder. Giving in with a sigh, he would retreat to the darkest corners of his study and return with a small brown box.

We would wait as fearfully as the geraniums while his grim face made us doubt our wish to view again this awesome souvenir of the war. Down would come the pendant lamp, throwing the room around us into darkness. Tentatively, as if the contents would bite, he withdrew the cotton-wool packing to reveal the horror we longed to see. A thumb, grey-blue with age, and splattered with dark clots of congealed blood lay there, so close we swore we could smell the decay. Transfixed by his stories of the savage battle we were totally unprepared for the sudden twitch of the thumb. Our belief had brought it to life, and our screams brought Gran running to chastise grandfather and lead us safely off to bed.

C.M.H.

BEHIND THE CAMERA

Llewelyn Edward Morgan began his life on 8 October 1885 in Ystradgynlais, Powys, the first child of Edward and Jane Morgan.

Llew's birthplace at Tir-waun, 1885.

Sunnyhill garden—Edward and youngest, Edith.

Jane's family, the Lewis's, were landlords of the Jeffrey's Arms, and were staunchly for 'King and Country'. Edward was similarly patriotic and proud of his direct descent from the Morgans of Tredegar, whose most famous family member was the buccaneering Captain Henry. However, it was Henry Morgan, King's servant and Governor of Jamaica, of whom he spoke, passing quickly over his years of plundering and piracy. Edward tackled his work as a miner with the same pride, respecting it as noble and dignified labour.

Due to the negligence of a servant girl, Jane had been partially crippled since the age of two, but this did not affect her superb organisation of the household, nor prevent her from having ten children; five boys and five girls.

As the little cottage in Tir-waun became cramped, her father loaned Edward enough money to build a house on the family plot next to the Jeffrey's Arms. On the crest of the hill facing south, the house was aptly named Sunnyhill, and here the Morgans settled to a secure and happy life.

Jane was a highly artistic woman, intelligent, and gifted with great skill in handicrafts. Her superbly detailed quilts were commissioned by Royalty and exhibited at the Louvre, in Paris. Her knowledge of Welsh flora and fauna was extraordinary and from a very early age the children were taught to draw from nature.

Jane and Edward Morgan in their garden at Sunnyhill.

Llew showed immediate ability, and because of his especially deep affection for his mother, he committed to memory the names of every plant she pointed out on their frequent country walks. While his father had several accidents underground, he would never have stayed away from mining. The male camaraderie and the sharing of extreme conditions were more than just a part of his life. As D. H. Lawrence notes in his essay, *Nottingham and the Mining Country:*

> . . . the continual presence of danger made the physical, instinctive and intuitional contact between men very highly developed. This physical awareness and intimate togetherness was at its strongest down the pit.

The author adds that he believed that the men brought these heightened feelings up with them, into the light.

In sharp contrast to the darkness and harsh conditions of their work, the beauty of nature made a deeper impression on the sensibilities of the miners. Edward's own appreciation seemed to be instinctive and contemplative, rather than intellectual. In winter especially, when shifts began and ended in the dark, any daylight and sunshine were to be savoured to the full.

Helping in the garden,
cousin Jeanette and sister Edith.

A favourite walk at Cwmynfaen, near Ystrad.

Country walks were precious, and the colliers of Ystradgynlais, one of the most westerly of the mining villages, took full advantage of the nearness of the Brecon Beacons. They might walk with their families, collecting berries or mushrooms, or, alone with their dogs, on the look-out for rabbits or kestrels.

If not out walking, the collier would be seen squatting on his heels on the Square watching the world go by, making his wry and philosophical comments to anyone who would listen.

Like many a miner, Edward loved his garden, though the hours he could spend there were limited. It was Jane, and then the children, who kept the eight acres behind Sunnyhill productive. There was a large orchard of apple and pear trees, an area of fruit bushes, and a well-stocked vegetable garden. In the field beyond, they kept a horse, which the children all got to ride, and more practically, a cow, pigs, geese and poultry. Surplus milk was sold in the village, as was the butter made from it, and the seasonal berries were preserved for winter use. Bees were kept for their honey—a hobby Llew continued in later life. This kind of self-sufficiency was necessary as the family grew, and it was also an accepted part of life at a time when 'easy money' was unheard of. One worked because there was need; each day had its duties, and everyone pulled their weight. There was a natural order to the week, according to the seasons.

Each Sunday saw Edward, on his only day off, dressed in his 'best', and acting as sidesman in the local church of St. Cynog's. This was another of his father's roles that Llew would emulate later. All the family would attend two services that day, with an afternoon Sunday school for the children. In addition, there was a weekly choir practice which each child attended as soon as he was deemed old enough to join the choir.

The love of music and singing was generally encouraged. It was strong in the Morgan home, and Jane saw to it that a piano was bought, and a tutor employed. Every week he would travel the fourteen miles from Swansea to spend several hours instructing the ten children.

The girls looked forward to their lessons, but the boys would have to be constantly goaded. At the first chance they would be off to the orchard, hiding in the foliage until the dreaded hours were over. Despite their prevarications, their mother continued to coach them towards a richer future than the narrow valley could promise.

As in all working-class families, each child, on reaching a certain age, acquired responsibility for some household chores. Llew, being the eldest, bore his with enthusiasm, so strong was his love for his mother. With the youngest, baby Edith, wound tight on his back in a Welsh shawl, he would get down on his knees to tackle the black-leading of the kitchen grate.

Only once was he embarrassed to be caught in such a humbling situation for a young boy, and that was when the Rector happened to call. As usual, he boomed his hearty greeting from the door, startling Llew to blushing, and the baby to tears. Humiliated, and unable to stop Edith's cries, Llew went in search of his mother, and was for several weeks thereafter a reluctant church attender.

The Rector, however, would have been astonished at the effect of his appearance on Llew. He was a frequent caller at the Morgan household, finding Edward and Jane interesting company. There was, of course, the added attraction of a glass of Jane's elderberry wine, or slice of blackcurrant tart.

The first positive sign that Jane's efforts would prove worthwhile was when Llew, at the age of eleven, was awarded a two-year County Scholarship to attend Ystalyfera Grammar School. Llew, however, although pleased that his family were proud of him, saw the event as symbolic. It seemed to toll the end of childhood and, therefore, of freedom.

Llew with his grandmother, Elizabeth.

What did lift his spirits was a splendid congratulatory gift from his grandmother of a Brownie box-camera. Llew was delighted but, as he lovingly observed every detail of his present, he could not have been aware that it would set the course of his life.

Immediately, he began to photograph his family, the garden, their prize sow, as well as village characters who were made to pose in 'natural' stances. Even at this early age, Llew showed charm and patience in handling his more difficult subjects. Both qualities were to stand him in very good stead.

During the week, when the camera was confiscated, he would use his long walks back and forth to school as preparation time for his new hobby. Taking the canal-bank route, he made mental notes of the flora, the birds,

Ynysgedwyn Ironworks, Ystrad.

dragonflies, the fish that surfaced from the murky depths, and the retired miner who sat every morning on that bridge over the river Tawe. The boy saw that his eyes, undimmed by coal dust, had that mixture of wonder and sadness, as if he saw beauty where no one else would have cared to look. This was what Llew yearned to capture on camera, nature and industry side by side.

But on he plodded, 'the whining schoolboy . . . creeping like a snail, unwillingly to school', until he reached Will the Smithy. There he stopped so long, composing the roaring flames and Will into his imagined picture-frame, that he was asked to lend a hand. He leapt at the chance and for a full hour engrossed himself in the world of work. On such a day he must have determined to escape from the classroom as soon as his scholarship ended. He would follow his father down the mines! His mind was made up. It was, of course, a disappointment to his parents, but they saw the signs of rebellion and knew that their insistence would only lead to trouble.

So it was that in 1899, at the age of fourteen, Llew left a promising school record to join his father and take the six-mile walk to Seven Sisters Colliery. There, along with five hundred others he began a ten-hour shift, to be followed by the return journey home; a six-day week, winter and summer.

Llew's first day proved to be unusually memorable. In one of the underground

The canal at Ystrad.

Seven Sisters Colliery.

'roadways' an escape of gas—a 'blower'—had been discovered. Contrary to regulations a safety-lamp had been opened and the gas fired. The flame, some four foot high, was used by the men as a splendid grill which allowed them to cook eggs and bacon on their polished shovels and enjoy pots of bubbling tea. Spiced as it was with the danger of discovery, the meals were a highlight of Llew's first days. It was with much regret that this group of friends watched the flame dwindle, to die out completely a fortnight later.

Now feeling part of the world of men, Llew was happy but, as his parents had feared, he soon met with an experience which an older man would not have survived. After a year of work he was riding alone on a 'journey' of empty tubs making its way down to the face in pitch blackness. His head caught an overhead beam and he was pitched over the side, grazing the side of his face on the outcrop. He lay huddled in the darkness, stunned, but safe, or so he thought. Suddenly, however, he was hit on the chest by the taut tail-rope which had swung across the track and was now in a position to pull up the laden tubs. With great difficulty he worked the cable over his head and slithered out, escaping its crushing weight.

Llew could now hear the approaching 'journey' and in great fear searched desperately along the walls for a safe niche. In his diary he wrote:

No welcome opening could I find. Instead my hands came into contact with the unprotected electric cables which worked the pumps. I was flung back against the steel rope which was swinging towards the centre of the 'roadway'. Ten tons of coal were making their way towards me. I felt blood trickling down my left side, but fear gave me the spur I needed to make my way forward. My hands closed around a post and I pressed myself behind its strength. There I stayed for three hours kept conscious by the passing rush of the 'journeys'. At the end of the shift a plate-layer found me and helped me up to safety.

Still determined to stay underground, Llew secured a job at Coelbren Colliery as a trainee electrician. When he qualified at the age of seventeen his parents felt relieved, but after a year's work he met with an accident that almost ended his life.

In the company of a young assistant he was installing a switchboard for a new pump and had given instructions that the power must be kept off. It was some time later, as he was about to connect the leads to the mains, that he was thrown backwards, grasping the live wires. Someone had not received his instructions.

A searing pain crossed his chest and he lost consciousness. His assistant grasped his coat to pull him away, but due to its wet condition, he received a severe shock. Llew explains:

Describing the scene later the boy said that I was enveloped in a blue light given off by the flames in my hands. The spasmodic contracting and relaxing of my muscles gave me a grotesque look which almost paralysed him with fear. Soon, the smell of burning alerted miners at the bottom of the slant. As they had to negotiate the passing 'journeys' it took them ten minutes to reach me.

Meanwhile I had been enjoying some near-death experiences in a huge building of nine storeys. The light was brilliant and changed colour as I rose through the levels to the final room. This was illuminated by a rose glow which showed up a magnificent door, through which I was keenly desirous of passing. I knew that once through that door, life's greatest secret would be revealed.

However, it was not to be, for I was hurled back by a mighty wind, back through all the rooms, and found myself lying on the ground, conscious again. One of the men had grabbed the tail of my coat and had dragged me to safety. I saw the brightness of miners' lamps and heard my name, as if from another planet. My hands were seared to the bone and my nerves badly shattered. This time my father was determined that I leave the mines forever.

During the healing of his hands and left arm, saved from amputation by the administrations of Marged Walters, a local herbalist, Llew had the leisure to read again. This helped to take his mind off the pain, and fill his time before the next treatment. This was hard to bear as Marged firstly bathed the exposed ligaments and bone in hot olive oil. Llew would faint away, but as he came around he saw his hands being soothed with herbal cream before the application of bandages. The recipe was Marged's secret and the effect was astounding. Within weeks a new flesh tissue had begun to form.

It was on his weekly walks to Marged's home in Cwmgïedd, a hamlet bordering Ystradgynlais, that Llew often saw a slim, dark-haired girl who returned his 'Good evening' with a shy smile. Blodwen Davies, then aged fifteen, had heard of the Morgan family with their Tory views and Church sympathies, ideas completely opposed to those of her own family, who were

Cwmgïedd.

staunch *Annibynwyr* (Independent), worshipping regularly at Sardis chapel.

Her father, Morgan Davies, was a fervent Liberal, a disciple of Lloyd George and Garibaldi. He had forged his own business from a talent as a carpenter and builder, and with his sons had taken on work for Adelina Patti at Craig-y-nos castle, and on St Peter's Church at Pontardawe.

Despite the difference in background, Blodwen and Llew were immediately attracted to one another and the die was cast. An unspoken decision prompted Llew to review his future and, giving in to his parents' pleas, he sat the University entrance examination. He was accepted at Exeter, his first choice and began his studies in 1907.

Llew now found himself in the very different world of English academia, but by the end of the first term he had proved himself and was respected by his tutors and popular with fellow students. While he excelled at his chosen subjects, Physics and Chemistry, he was also acknowledged as a highly accomplished draughtsman and sportsman.

For the first time in his life he played hockey, tennis and cricket, and by 1909 was captain of the college rugby team. He acquired a new confidence and looked quite the 'swell' when on vacation, dressed in white flannels, blazer, boater and spats, and enduring, with good humour, the 'Go on, you old Tory!' jibes of Ystrad boys.

Exeter University soccer team: Llew, front left.

Knowing that Blodwen's father was against the match, he advanced the friendship cautiously. One's politics were a serious consideration in those days, and it puzzled Morgan Davies that a mining family could be so confused and 'out of touch'. Still, he allowed the young couple to exchange letters, while Llew made as many visits home as possible. Because money was short, he would cycle from Exeter to Bath, pawn his bicycle for the train fare to Swansea, and reclaim it on his return. For the same reason he abandoned his expensive hobby of photography, and returned to his childhood favourite—painting. It was whilst recovering from breaking his arm in a rugby game that he completed a large oil painting of Tintern Abbey. Working only with his left hand, the effect was undiminished, and the canvas was acclaimed by both staff and students.

It was with great delight that his family heard of his graduation in Physics, and that he had secured a teaching post at Gurnos Junior School near Ystradgynlais.

Llew in tennis gear, 1909.

Engagement day, 1911.

With the news of Llew's graduation, Morgan Davies now openly admitted the qualities he had seen in Llew from their first meeting. He deemed him a reliable and hard-working young man, and was happy to grant permission for their marriage to take place. However, the thought of the wedding day, and of giving Blodwen away, was too much for him. A highly emotional man, he had decided that the duty had better be performed by his eldest son, Will.

With the Davies' budget stretched to the limit by the cost of wedding clothes and reception, Blodwen's mother, Marie, thought it best that she too should forgo attending the service, and instead keep her husband company at home.

The wedding took place on 27 December 1912 at St. Cynog's Church, Ystradgynlais,

with relatives from the Rhondda valley mixing with friends and family to fill the church to capacity. The wedding breakfast was held at the Davies's home, with the overflow being catered for next door in brother Jack's abode. There was roast beef with all the trimmings, but when it came to cut the cake, the cake itself could not be found. After a brief search, Marie was forced to serve another cake, one that had been intended for the neighbours. With 'face' saved, the celebrations continued, and it was much later, when the guests had gone, that the cake was discovered, secreted in a cupboard in Jack's house. The culprit was soon found to be one of Blodwen's sisters, who had long been jealous of her prettier sister and her courtship with a man of Llew's distinction.

Wedding day, 1912.

The married couple spent the night at Swansea's Metropole Hotel after seeing a performance of 'Rio Rita' at the Grand Theatre. The following morning they caught a train to London, a three-day treat paid for by Llew's parents.

Llew, of course, had his camera at the ready. Photographs were taken of pioneer Graham White, flying at Hendon, the animals at London Zoo, and of the opening events at the new White City Stadium. The days must have passed all too quickly for Blodwen who loved the excitement of city life and the different fashions and manners, all a far cry from the restricted ways of Cwmgïedd.

Honeymoon snaps, London.

On their return to Ystradgynlais they settled into a terraced house immediately opposite Sunnyhill, and while Blodwen began to organise the garden, Llew started work on building himself a dark-room. By the end of the first year the garden was planted with all the necessary fruits and vegetables, and an area fenced off for poultry and rabbits.

With his usual eye for *a picture*, Llew decided to photograph the animals as illustrations for some articles he had written for the English-language paper, *Llais Llafur* (The Labour Voice). They were immediately accepted for publication, and appeared under the title 'Diary of a Smallholder' and signed 'Leo'. With a humorous touch, Llew called the smallholding 'Ethiopia' and began the series of articles with a small stock of 'utility ducks, one pen of Leghorns, one pen of white Wyandottes', and adding as the year progressed, 'geese, rabbits, one turkey, a milking cow, a pony, and finally bees'. In fact, almost a replica of his mother's stock. The articles were meant to stimulate interest in self-sufficiency—the 'good life' as it is now thought of—and included 'Mrs. Leo's Tips on the Preserving of Fruits and Vegetables'.

In the same year, 1912, Llew was commissioned to illustrate, *Cerddi'r Mynydd Du* (Songs of the Black Mountain), by the poet, Gwilym ap Leishon. The book was well received, with Llew's photographs capturing the lyrical sentiments of the text. He greatly enjoyed the project which brought him into touch with writers and publishers, a wider world than his days at school could offer.

Teaching, however, was never to prove a problem for him. He was a natural communicator, and his enthusiasm for life and for his subjects easily transferred itself to the children. Often, on his weekend walks, a few eager pupils would accompany him, spotting wildlife through his binoculars and camera lens. During the following week they would wait impatiently for a private viewing of the prints, feeling a keen sense of having contributed to the magic.

He was now using a Leica, a camera which enabled him to make lantern slides for use in school. Subjects traditionally taught only through textbooks suddenly came to life with his illustrations of local history, geology and wildlife. The extra work involved in preparation ate into his evenings and often, way into the early hours of the morning. Blodwen must have been grateful for the family around her during these years, for company was to be had across the road at Sunnyhill, and at her parent's house in Cwmgïedd, a ten-minute walk away. Within two years, however, she had plenty to occupy her mind as she became pregant. Happy with the news, both she and Llew began to make plans for their first child, Llew working harder than ever to bring in some extra money.

In those days, and especially in a small Welsh community, when women were shy of being seen in an advanced stage of pregnancy, it seems strange that Blodwen agreed to join Llew, his sister, and brother-in-law, on a long walk to Llyn y Fan. The lake lies at the foot of Fan Hir, the long, mountain ridge north of Craig-y-nos castle, then the home of the opera diva, Adelina Patti. Later, on their return, Blodwen had told her mother how well she had felt; so healthy, that no thought of any ill-effect from the journey had entered her head.

Llew on location with his pupils.

Llyn y Fan Fawr.

When the four arrived at the lake, Llew took photographs of the dramatic escarpment which rises hundreds of feet above the water. It was as they began their descent to the road that Blodwen began to feel unwell, and by the time they reached Tafarn y Garreg, a hostelry on the main Swansea to Brecon road, she was in a very distressed state. As she rested, Llew went in search of help, and was lucky to see a horse and cart coming from a side road. It was driven by a business man from Ystradgynlais but, on hearing the problem, he refused to give even Blodwen a lift home.

Blodwen was never the kind of person to complain about personal discomfort or illness, her pride being quite strong, so that after a brief rest she was determined to walk the remaining six miles to Ystrad. Llew seethed with rage, and unbeknown to the others had attempted to wrest the reins from the driver who had declined to help his wife. A fight would inevitably have broken out had the man not driven off at some speed.

The following morning Blodwen went into labour and was delivered of a baby boy, two months premature. He was named Eric Ramsay after Ramsay MacDonald, the leader of the Labour Party, and brought with him only temporary joy. From birth he suffered from convulsions, and died when only six weeks old. Probably blaming herself for her irresponsible walk, Blodwen went into a long period of grieving and vowed that she would never have another child. His cream crocheted bootees, made by sister Blanche, and his tussore hankie were kept in a small box and were never to be used. It was 1914, and life would change dramatically for all Europeans when war was declared.

In the spring of that year, Llew's brother, Tom, a navy engineer, came home for a week's leave. He always joked that the journey from

Swansea docks to Ystradgynlais took longer than any of his world voyages.

As he relaxed at home, Tom's captain changed the schedule and all crew were told to be ready to sail on the next morning's tide. A telegram was sent to Tom late that afternoon, by way of Ystrad Post Office. The postmaster, in his position of absolute authority, decided that the message was of no great importance and could wait for the morning delivery.

When Tom read the telegram his ship had sailed, bound for a two-year trip up the Amazon. Bitterly disappointed, he sought another posting, and found himself caught, like thousands of others, in the grip of the First World War. For the rest of his life he was to suffer the after-effects of that most brutal conflict.

During Llew's years at Exeter he became increasingly aware of the difference between the living standards of the working classes in England and South Wales. During his first few months back home his political stance changed dramatically. He began to attend local Labour meetings and in a short time, with a few like-minded friends, he formed the first Swansea valley branch of the Independent Labour Party. They called themselves the Pioneers—the I.L.P. Scouts, as Ted, a keen scout member, nicknamed them—for their uniform of grey trousers and shirt was similar to his. The Pioneers chose a red neckerchief as a symbol of their left-wing sympathies.

As numbers grew, a hall was found for meetings, and it was here that Blodwen and the other wives organised fund-raising dances and bazaars. For such events the hall was always packed out, and while Blodwen took charge of the soft-drinks stall, her list of promised dances filled the rest of the evening. With his all-round enthusiasm for life, Llew loved to dance, especially the Lancers, and the Cotillion,

Llew's brother Tom, Royal Engineer.

Ted (Skip) and Frank, Llew's brothers, off to war.

though his style left something to be desired in his wife's book. Graceful as she was throughout her life, she preferred the more romantic waltzes.

These occasions proved both financially and politically successful. Plans to invite important speakers to the meetings were put forward, and it was Blodwen who proposed that it would be a respectful touch if the men wore bow-ties for special functions. However, she may have regretted her offer to make the ties as the membership was now up to two hundred. But with money from the funds, the red silk was bought and her volunteers went to work.

It must have been with great pleasure that Blodwen's father watched the turn-about in Llew's political philosophy, and he was there in the front row when his hero, Kier Hardie, came to address the branch. There then followed visits from Arthur Cooke, and other well-known Labour leaders, such as Minnie Pallister and Morgan Phillips.

After every special occasion there was supper for the guests at Blodwen's table. Hardie was her particular favourite, and she was happy to serve him with a third helping of her prized blackberry pie.

Ready for supper ar Merton.

Kier Hardie, a deeply-religious man, always began his meeting with a prayer, and when war broke out he led the pacifist wing of the I.L.P.

Llew now found himself more than ever in sympathy with him, and although not eligible for active service due to his mining accidents, he was not ashamed to make his objections to the war public.

With all his brothers eager to sign up, there were some difficult situations to be faced at Sunnyhill, but Llew was determined to declare himself a conscientious objector. When he presented his case to the board held at Brecon, his articulate and eloquent words caused quite a stir. He immediately volunteered for work with the Home Defence, duties to which he was fully committed.

Although the Morgan boys all returned safely to Ystrad at the end of the war, others were not so fortunate. Young cousins were lost in the fighting, and as the news of the horrors of trench warfare reached home, some, like Dick, Blodwen's eighteen year old nephew, worried themselves sick. Terrified of facing the battles, he would walk up and down the canal bank all night in the cold of December. Pneumonia ensued and he died within a few days.

Llew did all he could to raise morale, especially amongst his pupils whose fathers were stationed on the Western Front. He became a member of the Parish Council and Overseer of the Poor; he was elected Secretary of the Welsh National Poultry Association, and after a written examination became a Fellow of the Royal Horticultural Society. Using every spare moment of his day, he raised enough local interest to start an Angling Association, and a few years later became chairman of another home-grown group of antiquarians. Like all good communities Ystrad held together, sharing family sorrows and the few joys.

During a brief leave in London, Ted was struck down by the virulent flu epidemic of 1918. D. H. Lawrence, also on a few days stay in the city, contracted the same virus. Both, happily survived, but Ted was hospitalised and his family informed of the seriousness of his condition. Indeed, Llew and his parents made the long journey to London to see him. On arriving at the hospital they were all greatly relieved to be told that he was off the danger list, and as this was Edward and Jane's first visit to London, Llew decided to treat them to whatever took their fancy. Animal lover that he was, Edward chose the zoo, but before their visit both men went to the nearest barber's shop in Edgware Road.

As Edward was being 'lathered' he caught sight of a man taking his umbrella from the stand near the door. Shouting, 'Thief', he leapt from his chair and gave chase. Llew, half-way through being shaved, followed his father down the street but they lost the man as he slipped into the entrance of Marble Arch Underground station. Furious, they returned to the barber's shop, probably unaware of their soapy faces and the smiles of passers-by. Still bemoaning the loss of his umbrella, Edward's spirits were raised by the visit to Regent's Park and the zoo.

As Llew took photographs and entertained his mother, Edward wandered off, and when, after almost an hour, he had not returned, they began to worry. Checking all the obvious places first, Llew found his father admiring the pigs. Beaming with delight he declared them to be the best he had ever seen. Back home in Ystrad he would wax lyrical over the pigs, but when asked his opinion of London he would growl, ''Na dwll o le!' (What a hole of a place!)

The end of the war in 1918 was marked by a mixture of exultation and desolation. Ystradgynlais slowly returned to its village activities.

Craig-y-nos.

Always eager to increase his knowledge, Llew had obtained his City and Guilds First Class in Metalwork and Woodwork, and a Distinction in Advanced Drawing from Swansea College of Art.

In 1919 Adelina Patti died at her home in Craig-y-nos. Llew regretted that he had never photographed her. It was Blodwen who recalled that as a schoolchild she had been amazed when Patti had walked into their classroom to sing her favourite 'Home Sweet Home'. She also spoke of Patti's frequent carriage rides through Ystradgynlais, when, like Royalty, she would wave to the gathering crowds and throw pennies for the children.

After losing a son in 1914, Llew and Blodwen were delighted when their daughter Elizabeth (Betty), was born in 1920. This event changed Llew's outlook, and he set his sights on broadening his horizons. Ambitiously he applied for the post of Head of the Oxford Handicraft Centre, and was successful. With Blodwen's eager support, the family left the valley for a five-year stay in England.

Betty in the family album
designed by Llew.

Betty — Two months old.

The world has no such flower in any land,
And no such pearl in any gulf the sea,
As any babe on any mother's knee.

~ Swinburne ~

Betty and Mamma

Betty and aunty Ea.

Llew at Jesus College, Oxford.

Blodwen and sisters in a punt on the Isis, Oxford, 1922.

The "Kodak" Magazine

For Amateur Photographers

VOL. II. NO. 1   LONDON, JANUARY, 1924   PRICE TWOPENCE

"A November Scene"—The Winner

" WHERE THERE'S A WILL THERE'S A WAY !" AWARDED £5 5 0 IN THE NOVEMBER COMPETITION. TAKEN BY LLEW. MORGAN, YSTRADGYNLAIS, SWANSEA.

Kodak cover and First Prize: 'A November scene', 1924.

The mellow, Oxford life was very attractive to both mother and daughter. There were the swans to be fed on the Isis, treats to be had at the elegant tea shops, and new fashions to be enjoyed. Llew, however, was so engrossed in his new responsibilities that he had little time for leisure, or even for photography. With a better wage, however, he was able to invest in a half-plate camera which, along with his increased ability, produced a higher standard of professionalism. He won several 'Firsts' in *The "Kodak" Magazine* competitions and his work was featured on the front page on more than one occasion. But the Oxfordshire countryside, although beautiful, did not excite his imagination as did the wildness of Abergwesyn and the solitude of the Brecon Beacons.

At this time Llew was teaching older pupils, now concentrating on woodwork, metalwork, and technical drawing. However, he began to miss the study of nature and the enthusiasm of his younger pupils at Ystradgynlais. He soon realised that the hunger for learning was much greater in the mining communities of South Wales where education was regarded as a passport to a brighter future. As the years in Oxford passed he also began to miss the camaraderie of village life, the close community, and the sharing of joys and sorrows alike. The struggle towards social improvements were hardly in evidence in the Home Counties where a strong political stance seemed more a fashionable cult than a necessity.

In 1925, at the end of their fifth year in Oxford, fate took a hand when the centre was forced to close through lack of funds. Llew wrote to the Headmaster of Gurnos Junior School who had promised that he would always be welcomed back on the staff. His response was immediate and encouraging. So the Morgan family prepared for their move back to Wales, with only Blodwen showing regret. She had become accustomed to a style of life not known in the Swansea valley of that time. Oxford had been another world. From a

Return to village life. Ynysgedwyn Square, Ystradgynlais, 1925.

comfortable home they returned to the one small room at Sunnyhill until a suitable house was found a year later, again only a few doors from Llew's childhood home.

Llew now heard that as well as his old position at Gurnos, another more prestigious post, that of the Head of 'Arts and Crafts' was being offered at Maesydderwen County School. Only after happily accepting the latter was he told that his brother-in-law Alec Bounds, who had been unemployed since his return from active service in the 1914-18 War, had also been an applicant.

Alec Bounds had suffered amputation of the left leg during the war, and his wife, Llew's sister Lizzie, was now pregnant. In a move typical of his nature, Llew informed the education authority that he would prefer the Gurnos job. Lizzie was delighted when Alec was apppointed to the senior post, but she was never to enjoy the benefits. She died in childbirth three months later. Llew, however, never regretted his decision.

With his usual energy he took up his teaching post and was voted back on all the committees of which he had previously been a member. Later he joined both the Gower and Breconshire Preservation Societies. He was elated to be back on home ground and spent hours walking the hills near Craig-y-nos, waiting patiently for curlews, falcons, foxes, and rabbits to 'freeze' in front of his camera. The 'hides' he built were of sacking which he knotted and dipped in green dye. Seeming to have an instinct for predicting cloudless, moonlit skies, Llew would often plan to camp out on the hills at night, taking with him his most interested pupils. As his fame as a keen naturalist spread, farmers and gamekeepers would send him word if they happened to spot an unusual creature or incident.

It was Morgan Williams, whose responsibility it was to keep watch over game around Craig-y-nos, who told Llew that badgers had re-occupied a small cave in the limestone hill above the castle. So the small group set off,

Llew building a hide.

well-insulated in overcoats and mufflers, and reached their destination at 9.00 p.m. Settling down in the grass, they waited two hours before brock appeared from the cave. 'Caught in moonlight with his head high, sniffing the air for enemies, he looked a picture,' Llew wrote later in an article:

> Satisfied that he was safe, he began to groom himself; his long claws combing each side of his body. He then ambled slowly down the hill, and disappeared. Disappointed, thinking they had seen the last of him, the boys grew impatient. That, I decided, was the right time to bring out our 'midnight feast'. With the discomfort of lying on bare ground eased a little by the food, we were all soon entertained by a sight not experienced by

many. The badger was returning, but crawling slowly upwards as if in difficulty.

As he came into the strong moonlight, we noticed that under his abdomen, held sound between his hind legs, was a load of bracken. He was climbing by only using the sheer strength of his fore-legs, and, of course, his determined will. When he reached the cave he let go his bounty, and went back down the hill.

Five times he made this journey, and when he thought the pile of bracken sufficient for his needs he pulled it inside the cave. It was the male who was establishing a home in anticipation of a mate coming to join him there.

Delighted by their experience the boys made the return journey to Ystrad, and we were all restored by the sweet aroma of bacon and mushrooms waiting for us at my home.

Llew sent the article to *The Countryman*, and was rewarded with publication and numerous letters of interest in the sighting. These he always replied to fully, thereby building up quite a network of like-minded acquaintances.

One of the photographs he had taken of Blodwen at this time was of her gathering the edible snails which she kept. The idea of rearing *escargots* was suggested by a French woman who lived in the village. 'Full of protein and vitamins,' she had announced and had taught Blodwen the simple process. The photograph was of a very attractive young woman holding a basket of snails, and it duly

Blodwen with snails.

appeared in a national newspaper, with her name given as 'Miss B. Morgan'. Within a week a letter from a Yorkshire farmer arrived at the Morgan household. He declared himself so struck with love for Blodwen that he must propose marriage, and offered to send her the rail fare to Harrogate. There he would meet her, and escort her to his farm which, according to the letter, sounded very substantial.

The incident annoyed Llew. Blodwen, on the other hand, was secretly flattered, but she made Llew write a letter of explanation to her admirer, which he duly did. No more was heard from the lonely Yorkshireman, and life continued happily in Primrose Villa.

Their daughter Betty was now five, and had settled quite contentedly after her early days in Oxford. Still remembering feeding the swans and watching the trains arrive at Oxford, she was now content to play with her twenty-one first cousins.

One of Llew's most popular evening classes was in wireless making, and he must have been held responsible for the clearing of many a dinner-table to make room for soldering equipment, condensers, and the innards of a wireless. One of his keenest pupils was his brother-in-law, Will Morgan, who, on finding that he could 'pick up' Cologne, Stuttgart and Poste Parisien, would send his daughter with the exciting news, full-pelt to tell Uncle Llew. On re-telling the message however, the latter station had become 'Poster Parry John', and this became a long-standing family joke.

With his by now renowned enthusiasm, Llew had built for himself the best wireless set in the valley, and on her fourth birthday Betty was photographed receiving her 'Greetings from Auntie' direct from Alexandra Palace. It was one of the first national transmissions from the BBC.

The Oxford years had certainly broadened Llew's outlook, and he now thought nothing of driving the many miles to Machynlleth or Montgomery to deliver evening lectures, even after a full day's teaching. Whether the subject

The wireless class. Llew standing, right.

Betty tunes in to her birthday greeting.

was poultry-keeping, archaeology, or photography he was determined to entertain his audiences, for whom he had the greatest respect. During the long, and often, cold return journeys, he would plan his next day's school-work, and would frequently spend a few hours before dawn processing a series of prints.

Although the I.L.P. had been absorbed into the Labour Party during the war, Llew, as local chairman, worked diligently in support of the miners' claims for better working conditions and higher wages. Having run smoothly up to 1918, the mining industry was now being threatened by imports, ironically, from the coalfields of a defeated Germany. The miners demanded nationalisation of the industry, an idea which had been endorsed by the wartime government. During the early 1920s, however, with the competition from abroad, the industry and the country in general was in the grip of a depression. Britain was a far cry from Lloyd George's promise of a 'land fit for heroes'.

To stall the decline, the government announced a reduction in miners' pay, and the enforcement of longer working hours. They also withdrew their support for nationalisation. Feelings ran high, and Arthur Cooke, miner's agent for South Wales, coined the slogan: 'Not a penny off the pay, not a minute on the day.' It became the battle cry of the Miners' Federation as other unions rallied in support.

On 3 May 1926 the T.U.C. announced a General Strike as all pits closed and transport came to a halt. Llew put his car at the disposal of the party, and at the headquarters a soup kitchen was set up to provide food for the colliers' families. Prayers were said in chapels and churches for a speedy end to the strike, but while they had promised all-out support, the T.U.C. were already discussing lower wages with the government. On 13 May the union announced the end of the strike, and the miners were left alone to fight for improved conditions.

On a stringent diet the miners survived until November, when, envisaging greater hardships as winter approached, they decided to return to work. A small miracle that occurred at that time is still remembered today. A young boy, playing with friends on the banks of the river Tawe, sustained a cut on his foot. With help he made his way to the home of Dr. Walsh who, on cleaning the wound, removed coal dust. As the word spread, dozens of miners and their families made their way to the spot where the accident had occurred and dug up quantities of 'black gold'. Coal houses, sheds, even baths were filled before pit managers heard the news. If they could have done anything at all, it was too late—the river had yielded its gift.

As the government had warned, many of the smaller pits closed, and seeing only darker times ahead, hundreds of families decided to emigrate. One of Llew's close friends, Gwilym Jones, a tenor of national acclaim, moved to Chicago and found work in the Ford motor industry. In the space of two years he had saved enough money to have his wife and their six children join him in a better life.

Arthur Cooke (centre), miners' agent, in Ystrad Park addressing a meeting.

'Hands Off Russia': a meeting in Ystrad Park to resolve the conflict between the left and right wing of the Socialist Party over intervention in Russia.

The population of South Wales declined and during the years of privation the number of cases of consumption and rickets increased greatly. Because the Tory government had failed to support a loyal and decent group of workers, left-wing sympathies were strengthened. In the hamlet of Ynys, bordering Ystradgynlais, the home of a number of Communist Party members, strong backing had been given to the miners' cause. Here, poverty was at its most severe, with regularly reported cases of T.B.

The Labour Party in Ystrad did all it could to restore belief in the good life. Outings in

'Mr. Morgan's' car were a treat for many of the village children during this period of privation and Llew used the day trips as an opportunity to vary his photographic subject matter.

During the late 1920s and early 1930s competitions for amateur photographers became popular in national newspapers and magazines alike. Llew dismissed the 'craze' of the snapshot as too commercial for his liking, but encouraged by Blodwen he agreed to 'have a go'.

While taking his usual 'twenty winks' after dinner his mind would churn over with ideas. Springing to his feet he would surprise the family with strange requests for fashionable hats or 'baggy pants'. Having admired 'beach pyjamas', then the vogue in magazines, Blodwen was delighted to 'run-up' two pairs. Though mother and daughter thought them rather incongruous outfits for mushrooming or river-fishing they nevertheless posed happily as Llew 'snapped' away. As usual, when it came to photography, he was correct and the proof came in the form of many First prizes.

Blodwen and Betty on the beach.

These outings were the perfect excuse for a picnic, a meal which was planned to placate the nerves, for Llew had only a vague idea where they were heading. The journey was made up of a series of stops as Llew came across one suitable subject after another. Promising to return in 'just a tick', he would dash off with camera at the ready. 'Just a tick' would often stretch to a good twenty or thirty minutes, but more often than not he would return with a triumphant smile.

Life in the Morgan household now became hectic as plans to engage the right 'models' had to be made, sometimes, weeks ahead. Betty's friends leapt at the chance of a day out, but they soon learnt that it was not all going to be 'sweetness and light'.

Betty surprises her friends at Horton.

Llew was exacting as a director, making everyone pose a dozen times for each 'shot'. The children, however, thought it just like being 'in the pictures', especially as Mrs Morgan, as leading lady, was as temperamental as any Hollywood star: 'Now, lift your left hand to your eyes,' Llew would say, looking through the lens, 'and tilt your head slightly to the right.' 'I'm doing it,' Blodwen would say with a long sigh. 'You're not!' he would shout in response. 'I am,' she would insist. When the print was finally brought from the dark-room as proof-positive that she had *not* been 'doing it', Blodwen would ignore the evidence!

Llew's temper was short and sharp and perhaps quite justified as he strove to produce the perfect print. But the occasional flare-ups were soon forgotten when family and friends saw their faces beaming from the front pages of the national press, above picture captions

Children on the beach, Gower.

Hiking days with the Morgan's dog, Buddy.

such as 'Happy Days'—First Prize to Llew E. Morgan'. Indeed, each model was given a print of their day's 'work', and would always wait eagerly for the competition results. When Llew was victorious, the local shop ran out of newspapers in record time. It was a welcome distraction from the often hard conditions of valley life.

In the early 1930s hiking became popular, so for a topical 'snap' Llew kitted the family out with khaki shorts, shirts, rucksacks and tough shoes. The provider was his brother 'Skip', a scoutmaster, who was to be honoured as a Queen's Scout and later with an O.B.E.

In Skip's book, *Still Glow the Embers* (1976) there is an account of a not so successful day of photography:

> Wanting to photograph a kite on its nest Llew asked a friend, Ernie Perkins, to come along and help him with the venture. It entailed carrying the

necessary equipment over a mile of rough ground and then lowering Llew, sitting on a looped rope, over the edge of a precipice. It was an unusually hot Spring day, causing a foul smell to rise from the occupied nest. Ernie was instructed to keep well clear so that the parent would return to feed the young.

Not having slept after his night shift, and lying under the blazing sun, Ernie soon fell into a deep sleep, and was not to wake until darkness had fallen.

In a panic, he stumbled back to where he could hear feeble cries for help, and began to pull Llew to safety. In some distress, the victim threatened all kinds of revenge, but Ernie retaliated: 'Half a mo, Llew, you're not up yet!', and lowered the rope several feet.

The journey home was in total silence, but it wasn't long before they were rambling the hills together again. Llew wasn't one to bear a grudge for long,

and, as usual, the photographs were a great success.

Although Llew had done little painting since his University days, he had an artist's eye for composition, lighting and tone. Colour work was becoming popular but was expensive, and, of course, had to be sent away for processing. Llew felt that if the end result was to bear his signature he must have complete technical control of the developing process. Black and white work was his forte, but when the *Austin Magazine* chose his photograph of Blodwen and Betty beside the Austin Seven as a front cover illustration he allowed the print to be tinted.

As tolerant as he could be with human models, Llew had infinitely more patience with animals. Often, he would find a wounded creature unable to fend for itself. It would be brought home and nursed back to health by Blodwen, to be returned when recovered to the exact spot where it had been found.

The Austin Magazine, 1929 and the photograph awarded the First Prize at the National Eisteddfod, Treorchy, 1928.

Country idyll—First Prize, National Eisteddfod, Liverpool, 1929.

Children playing on a swing—First Prize, National Eisteddfod, Treorchy, 1928.

His animal photographs won him First Prize at the National Eisteddfod of Wales at Treorchy in 1928. In addition, he was also awarded Firsts in the sections devoted to 'Buildings', 'People' and 'Lantern Slides'.

These successes in all sections were repeated in the National Eisteddfod held in Liverpool in 1929.

In addition to his photographic work, Llew was still writing articles for the *South Wales Voice*, often in a satirical vein and covering local politics. Calling himself 'Do Consilium', he propounded schemes for improving the neighbourhood. The following is an extract:

> Roadways:—I suggest putting all the hills giving ingress to, and egress from Ystradgynlais, end to end, switchback fashion, so that traffic descending one hill could clear the next. This would entail no cost, as faith, as we know, can move mountains . . .
>
> Lighting:—Some people think that public lighting of roads is unnecessary, but, I doubt it. Under cover of darkness we Christian people are apt to say 'goodnight' to our bitterest enemies . . .

> Pollution:—It is well-known that the River Tawe is badly polluted. What with the coal washed down from Abercrave, and the oil pollution further down the valley, spontaneous combustion might easily take place. Should the Tawe catch fire, and threaten Teddy Bear bridge, I suggest that the canal be re-routed to put out the blaze. Another outcome would be that fresh grilled fish would be so readily available as to seriously affect the fish and chip industry . . .
>
> Bill Posting:—During the recent storms the cinema hoarding was destroyed, thereby improving the attractiveness of the Square in one blow. I suggest that if such ugly hoardings are necessary, let them be put up on Palleg hill where they might also serve as sheep shelters. All those not able to read the cinema advertisements in this very paper can obtain necessary exercise by an early morning walk up the appointed hill.

He also suggested that a boxing ring be placed on the Cross to be used by candidates standing at local elections, and thereafter, to stage the contests indulged in by the members of the local council. His colums were always popular, but time was always pressing, and photography was his priority.

In the mid 1930s Llew became a founder member of the Wallace Heaton Photographic Postal Club, which aimed to give constructive criticism to amateur enthusiasts. Each month thirty prints would arrive at Merton for appraisal, and Llew would give his full concentration to advising on all aspects of the work. He maintained that he learnt much by studying the efforts of others. A few members became lifelong friends, and were always welcome to visit Merton, and 'talk photography'.

Eric Hosking, the renowned nature photographer, greatly admired Llew's sophisticated printing and developing skills as well as his technical expertise in repairing and servicing his cameras. They met when Llew took yet another First in the Fishguard National Eisteddfod, 1936, which drew entrants from the whole of Great Britain. Over the years he had won thirteen First Prizes, but Hosking's praise was greatly valued. In his words, 'Llew combined the talents of a true creator, being a great craftsman and an even greater artist.'

At the Eisteddfod meeting Llew formed what was to prove another rewarding friendship, with a young BBC broadcaster by the name of Wynford Vaughan-Thomas. He was preparing notes for a future programme on the 'Saith Maen', the seven ancient stones erected by prehistoric man to point the way across the Beacons, and in Llew he had found the perfect guide. Wynford was, of course, invited to stay at Merton, and with their love of Wales, the historical and physical landscape, a lasting bond was formed.

Wynford became a frequent weekend guest at Merton where Blodwen, although fond of him, was quite taken aback by his smiling request for *three* eggs with his breakfast bacon, and three sugars in each of his many cups of tea. However, she had an ulterior motive in

making him as comfortable as possible. Her younger sister, Elvira, though very attractive, was still unmarried, and had taken quite a liking to the visitor. Blodwen would have given him six sugars if it would have sweetened his interest. Unfortunately, Wynford and Llew were either deeply engrossed in political conversation, or were out, tramping miles across the hills. As Blodwen saw her dream disperse she rationed Wynford's sugar to two lumps.

It was in 1937 that Llew, as Secretary of the N.U.T., was obliged to attend a conference in London, and decided to take his family along as a 'treat'. Blodwen was delighted at the chance to see the big stores that she had only read about. Each afternoon they met Llew for tea at the newly opened Lyon's Corner House near Marble Arch, where the famous 'Nippies', waitresses in black dresses topped with white aprons and frilly starched caps, served. Betty was very impressed by them as she was by a group of ladies at the next table, who were daintily eating their pastries with tiny forks. Determined to try and master this skill only brought her shame, for the cream shot out of her choux pastry and flew across the table.

Later, the family would stroll through the streets towards Leicester Square, but on one particular evening, Llew, who had participated in a fiery debate at the conference, decided he would prefer a quieter route. As they walked leisurely, they came across a group of Labour supporters on a street corner. They were handing out leaflets and naturally, Llew took one, but before they had walked more than a few steps, there were angry shouts and the sound of scuffling. Llew hurried his wife and daughter into a doorway, and turned to investigate the cause of the row. A gang of Oswald Moseley's 'Blackshirts' had descended on the Labour men, and were pushing them from their 'spot'. Without hesitating, Llew rushed to their defence, and was in the thick of what turned out to be a nasty brawl. Alarmed, Blodwen hurried Betty along the street with a 'Ladies can't stand on the streets in London' explanation. When Blodwen looked back, all she could see was a mass of men fighting and Llew's own Homburg hat flying up in the air. She retraced her steps and saw the police arrive with the 'clanging' of a 'black maria'. To her horror she saw Llew being hauled with the Labour boys into the van which sped off through the traffic.

Blodwen pushed her way through the crowd of onlookers and asked a policeman where she could find her husband. 'At the nearest station where he will be charged,' came the reply, and she was advised to go back to her hotel and wait for him.

For Blodwen, holding on to the battered Homburg hat and placating Betty, it seemed hours before Llew returned, apologetic, but 'railing' against the behaviour of the police. The Labour men had been branded trouble-makers, and fined for causing a breach of the peace, while the Blackshirts were seen as vigilantes. He was determined to write to all the national press about the incident, which he thought had contravened the laws of civil-rights, but his letters were published in only two newspapers, the *Daily Herald* and the *Daily Worker.*

Within months of his return home, however, politics took second place to his other passion—geology.

The hills around Craig-y-nos.

The hills around Craig-y-nos were known to be rich in caves. One, called Eglwys Caradog (Caradog's Church), was said to be the place where the Welsh prince preached Christianity in the fourth century after his seven-year captivity in Rome.

Excavations carried out since the 1920s had been slow and sporadic, but when, in the 1930s, a huge fall of weathered rock exposed a maze of tunnels, Sir Mortimer Wheeler, then Keeper of the Department of Archaeology at the National Museum of Wales, Cardiff, was called to the site. There was great local interest and Llew offered his help as photographer. With his knowledge of the area he proved of invaluable assistance.

Beyond the Lakes, Dan yr Ogof caves.

In the company of Sir Mortimer he crawled through an eighteen-inch tunnel for about fifteen feet, before they had headroom. They had reached a vast chamber of sparkling stalagmites and stalactites with lime carbonate walls which glistened in the torchlight.

The earth floor was found to be a treasure trove of human and animal bones, with bronze artifacts later dated at around 1300 B.C. These were painstakingly passed along to the narrow entrance, placed on stretchers, and carried down to the nearby Gwyn Arms.

The proprietors, the Prices, had been close friends of the Morgans for many years, so there was no problem in asking the regular patrons to drink in the kitchen while the two public rooms were used for the laying out of the bones.

All the findings were photographed by Llew, labelled and packed. They included Viking rings and Roman coins, and as Llew had kept detailed notes of the venture he was asked to compile the first Dan yr Ogof

Members of the Mendip Society with Dr Savory of the National Museum of Wales outside the Bone cave.

Cover of the first guide to Dan yr Ogof caves, 1938.

brochure in 1938. He and Sir Mortimer became staunch friends, and kept in touch for many years.

Llew was commissioned by the owners of the cave to write a detailed description of the locality and its history up to the 1930s:

The District

> In the year 1879 the great *prima donna*, Madame Patti, made her home at Craig-y-nos Castle. She was a woman of the world who had travelled extensively and who had been a welcome visitor at many a beautiful mansion in many a beautiful country. She had been in search of a home—'a home sweet home,' and her choice fell on Craig-y-nos. To her, the valley was a valley of romance, a valley whose mountain sides would echo and re-echo the notes of her unrivalled voice.

The valley is the same to-day, but the grand voice is still. The great castle has become the centre of healing. The pure air, uncontaminated by the smoke and the grime of the lower industrial areas, is balm to the weakened lungs of the town dweller. Cribarth and the Task, two rugged bastions of grey limestone guarding the entrance, are still there, home of the red fox, the badger, the buzzard, and the raven.

Over the Cribarth in prehistoric times ran a ridgeway, probably a continuation of that on the Drum mountain which is marked with many cairns where the dead of those days lie buried. This ridgeway continued to the Cribarth, then passed along the side of the valley, crossing the river Haffes first, and the river Tawe Fechan next, until it reached the stone circle below the slopes of Fan Hir. Here it crossed the Tawe and continued in the direction of Castle Drake and the Castle Mound at Trecastle.

Immediately beyond Cribarth and on the ridgeway, here dotted with cotton grass, lies the Saith Maen, a group of seven stones erected by prehistoric man to point the way. Several standing stones set up for the same purpose mark the track from there onwards. The stone circle is a small one of twenty-one stones, with a large old red sandstone monolith outside. In its neighbourhood are the remains of hut circles, and a cairn locally called Bedd-y-Cawr (the Giant's Grave).

From the Trecastle road, a thirty minutes easy walk brings one to Llyn y Fan Fawr. This lake sustains no fish life. Even as far back as 1687 there were no fish in it. It was in this year that a huge overhanging rock fell into the pool, flooding both the Usk and the Tawe valleys and doing considerable damage.

The lake is surmounted by Fan Foel,

Saith Maen.

2,603 feet. A wonderful sight awaits the person who climbs the path leading from the lake to the heights above. On clear days the Bristol Channel and the coasts of Somerset and Devon are easily seen, and a panorama of flat country, and of hills and mountains stretching north to Plynlimon and Cader Idris delights the eye. About a mile and a half away Llyn y Fan Fach can be seen. This lake is renowned for the legend, 'The Lady of the Lake.' It is the story of a lake maiden who was enticed from the depths by a mortal, he having promised her father that he would not strike her thrice without cause. Unfortunately, he un-wittingly failed to keep to his promise and she returned to the lake. Her descendants, so tradition states, were the Meddygon Myddfai, who were well-known physicians.

In a MS on Breconshire at the British Museum a writer, writing in 1695 and mentioning Fan Hir, the mountain culminating in Fan Foel, adds: 'There is also a greate Poole on each side of it which makes it most dreadfull presenting Death on all sides . . . which Pools are worth ones noteing, the one called Llynllwch Sawthey for its abundance of fish of all-sorts especially for its troutes which are dayly taken in greate store, but the poole is in Carmarthenshire, the other of a contrary nature in this county called of the Hill Llyn-y-fan-hir hathe no fish attalle in't nither will any fish being put into it live, but as soon as they have tasted of this water turne up there Silver Bellies and dey.'

Another reservoir lies east of these pools over Cefn Cul, and on the Brecon road. This is Crai and it supplies Swansea with fresh water. This pool is well stocked with trout, and fishing is possible there.

Llew then goes on to describe the 1912 visit to the caves by the owners of the land, the Morgan brothers of Tŷ-Mawr, Abercrave. They found an opening large enough for them to crawl through, and on reaching the other end of the passage were able to stand in a cavern which was well above the water course. With their way blocked by a large pool, they determined to return the following day with materials enough to construct a small craft.

The Dagger Chamber.

The Three Nuns.

On discovering further caves and lakes, a coracle was brought from Carmarthen, and using another new route they were able to negotiate their way deep into the hillside. Here they found their passage blocked by a tremendous underground waterfall. Having to return to the entrance, no more excavations were undertaken until 1937. Llew goes on to explain:

> The present day visitor to the cave will not experience any of the difficulties and dangers of the intrepid cavers who first entered it. The cave is now rendered accessible to all. The debris, accumulated through the ages, has been removed.

Cement or sand renders the floor easy to walk on, and neither the shoes nor the clothes of visitors need be soiled. Electric light, generated by turbines turned by the issuing water, illuminates the passages and vast chambers and displays the wonders these contain.

Stalactite and stalagmite formations are numerous and take on interesting and grotesque shapes. Some of these are beautifully coloured owing to the presence of minerals in the strata above.

A few yards from the entrance may be seen the Frozen Waterfall, a huge mass of stalactite deposit coloured a vandyke brown hue by peaty matter brought down from the moors above. Farther in, on the left, is perched a White Parrot, the result of ages of effort by the greatest sculptor of all time—Nature.

Near by, a continuous stream of water resembling a shower bath, reaching from ceiling to floor, shows up in the electric light like dozens of crystal wires varying in size and number according to the weather prevailing on the hills above.

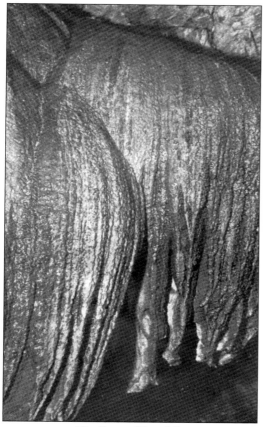

The Frozen Waterfall.

Ahead, silhouetted against the light, is a Wolf's Head with jaws agape. This is carved out of the solid rock which hereabouts is fretted into most fantastic and weird shapes. On the left are calcite formations of flint-like appearance, the

top and bottom masses joined together by thin, pencil-shaped stalactites.

Excavation work, with the support of the Mendip Exploration Society, would have continued had not events in Europe taken centre-stage. Work was brought to an immediate halt by the outbreak of the Second World War.

Llew had been teaching for twenty-seven years and now watched his first pupils sign-up for active service. He was appointed Special Constable and Air Raid Warden. The Ministry of Agriculture, who had always valued his work, asked him to prepare a series of talks on poultry and rabbit-keeping. As food shortages were likely, it was vital that every householder should be encouraged to keep productive animals. Offices in Brecon and 200 miles away in Mold were made available to Llew, who welcomed the additional responsibilities and travelling with his usual enthusiasm.

Conscientious as he was, he made plaster models of the innards of poultry and rabbits, demonstrating the effects of tumours and the most prevalent diseases. These he made into a comprehensive series of lantern slides.

In 1943 he was appointed Area Organiser for Wales and the Marches, using offices in Cardiff as a base. Betty, with her architect husband, Howel Hopkin, was now living in the city, and Llew would often stay the night with them, instead of driving home in the 'black-out'. But, as Cardiff was the target of frequent air-raids, Llew was always thankful to return to the comparatively peaceful and normal life in Ystradgynlais, despite the Ack-Ack station in Cwmgïedd, and two near misses from German planes as they retreated from Swansea.

It was the area's comparative safety which drew the young Polish artist, Josef Herman, and his wife, Catriona Macleod, to the village. A refugee from Warsaw via Brussels, Jo had arrived in Glasgow, met Catriona, one of the Macleods of Skye, and eloped with her to London. Wartime London was no place to be,

Llew, as special constable, with Betty.

especially as they were expecting their first child. The couple were offered hospitality by Peg and Dave Williams, while Jo set about converting a disused 'pop' works into a studio and living accommodation. What he envisaged would be a brief stay turned into eleven years.

Blodwen and Llew, who took to the young couple immediately, helped them set up home. 'Jo bach', as he was soon called by the villagers, began work, portraying the miners and their families. Through his artist's eyes he saw 'violet roofs at the foot of green hills. Pyramids of black tips surrounded by cloud-like trees the colour of a dark bottle' (*A Welsh Mining Village*, 1962).

The only photographs of Jo at work were taken by Llew, who didn't have the patience to 'sit' in return. A portrait was begun but it was never completed by Jo.

As the artist's fame spread, admirers from London and abroad found their way to the Welsh valley, and the extra china and cutlery needed could always be borrowed from Blodwen.

Jo's painting of a miner.

The writer, Leo Koenig, Jo Herman, and Llew at Merton, 1948.

Open invitations to supper at Merton were always taken up, with conversation extending to the small hours.

In his *Notes from a Welsh Diary* (1993) Jo recalls 'walking with Llew all the way from Ystradgynlais, we talked about the strange attraction of isolated places':

> Llew was what I would call a down-to-earth photographer. He trusted his eye, his camera, and the dark-room where he developed his prints.
>
> His criteria were quite simple: the subject had to be rendered as it presented itself to his eyes. Because of this his photographs have a strong documentary quality, and are thus quintessential to the understanding of the everyday life of Wales.
>
> As reality is rich and varied there was no problem of him getting short of subjects. Outside this he followed no preconceived theory.
>
> The sheer quantity of his work is amazing, considering how self-critical he

was. In spite of his strong commitment to his craft he remained a modest man.

I remember him best as everyone could see him, a short stocky man with a camera hanging on a leather strap down his chest. This alone distinguished him from others in the streets of Ystradgynlais.

His grey hat and raincoat was the same as others in the street, in fact, in any crowd he was like so many others. You had to know him more intimately to share his knowledge of Wales and the things specifically Welsh.

My frequent chats with him remain inscribed in my memory with the echoes of his quiet voice.

It was also through Peg and Dave that Llew met David Martin, author of the novel, *Tiger Bay* (1947). He became a frequent visitor at Merton, never tiring of discussing with Llew his experiences during the Spanish Civil War. He had then been foreign correspondent for *Reynold's News*, a national paper with left-wing sympathies.

Another character who brightened the 1940s was Joan Littlewood, whose company performed at the village Miners' Welfare Hall. The building had been erected through the instigation of Llew's friend, James Griffiths, a local man who later became M.P. for Llanelli, and Secretary of State for Wales. Joan was famous for her left-wing theatrical productions.

In 1943 Llew was asked to write and present a nature series for BBC radio. It was so successful that he continued this freelance work for seventeen years, covering subjects from botany to history.

Although all thoughts were centred on events in Europe, attention was more than a little diverted when the film director Humphrey Jennings chose Cwmgïedd as the setting for his production of *The Silent Village*. This feature film was based on what was then recent events in Lidice, a Czechoslovakian village invaded by the German army. Every man and boy had been slaughtered, and the women sent to concentration camps.

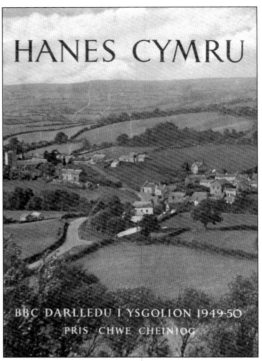

BBC pamphlet, *Hanes Cymru*.

As Jennings' Crown Film Unit seemed to take over the village, volunteers for 'extra' work abounded. The portrait photographer, Walter Bird, was there to take the 'stills' and struck-up a lifelong friendship with Llew. His London-based 'Studio Roye' was renowned for the quality of the work he produced. Merton's dark-room became Bird's second home where Llew's new enlarger proved indispensable for 'blowing up' the stills.

The film's premier was at the Astoria cinema, immediately opposite Merton. Years before, Llew had been asked to buy into the business when the Page brothers had wanted to sell. Much as he would have enjoyed the venture, money was always short, and the terms too risky. He attended the premier in the company of Blodwen, and a few months later, in 1943, *The Silent Village* went on general release.

So taken was Bird by the countryside of South Wales, that he and his wife bought a house near Trapp, Llandeilo, and remained staunch friends of the Morgans.

There was only one occasion in Llew's life when he was so paralysed with fear that he would not have been able to press the shutter of his camera, had he been holding one at the time.

In October 1944 Llew, on Ministry of Agriculture duty, had driven to Downend, near Bristol to deliver a lecture. It was at the invitation of the local Poultry Keepers' Club, who would normally have had him stay the night at one of the member's homes. On this particular night, however, no such hospitality was possible, and alternative accommodation was found at a very good hotel—a rather grand Georgian manor.

After a successful lecture and a light supper, Llew made his way back to the hotel, only to be met by a manservant who seemed to know nothing about a room booked in his name. Llew was asked to wait in the baronial hall while the man made enquiries with the management. He did not return for some time, and Llew heard noises from above, as if a room were being hurriedly prepared for him. On his return, the man explained that a room could be made available provided that it was required for one night only. When Llew confirmed that he only wished to stay the night, he was shown upstairs to a small, sparsely furnished space which had an interconnecting door into the next room blocked by a large chest of drawers. With no heater in the room, Llew made quick work of getting into bed, hoping that his tiredness would send him into an untroubled sleep. This, however, was not to be. The place was unnaturally icy, and after a few hours the temperature dropped noticeably. Turning towards the window, he hoped to see the first signs of dawn but everything was pitch black.

It was at that moment that Llew became aware of a presence in the room, and fully believing that someone had entered, he turned to see a human face hovering near the door. As he later wrote:

> The face glowed with a strange light. The complexion was ruddy, the eyes, dark, the nose, bulbous. The head was covered by a black cowl which curved down over the shoulders. All else was obscured by the gloom. Fascinated, and horrified, I moved slowly into a sitting position, remembering that at my side was a table-lamp. The ghost, for I was now convinced that that was what I was looking at, continued to stare at the inter-connecting door. He moved towards it, and then, as if changing his mind, turned full towards me, and started to advance.
>
> It was then that my nerve broke, and uttering some incoherent sound, I reached, fumbling for the lamp, found the switch and turned it on. Even this small light dazzled me, but its soft glow was so welcome a relief. I dared to turn and survey the room. Everything was as it was, nothing out of place—an ordinary space.
>
> I spent the rest of the night propped up in bed, turning the light on and off, wondering if the monk-like figure would return in the dark intervals. As dawn brightened the sky, I felt restored but ready to sleep. I wondered if the owners of the house knew of the hauntings. That would explain their reticence in not letting the room for more than a night.
>
> I had read of some psychic happenings, and had long been interested in the experiences of Conan Doyle, but had always found it hard to believe in many spiritual events. Now, however, as I drove home, I knew that ghosts appear more tangible than the transparent, misty individuals described in fiction.

On arriving at Merton he went straight to bed, and only after a few days did he recount his adventure to the family. Knowing him to be a soundly practical man, there was no doubting that he had had an experience which defied logical explanation.

In 1945, following the end of hostilities with Germany, V.E. Day was experienced as a time of mixed emotions for those who had survived and those who had lost family and friends. In Ystrad there was a feeling of great relief, with flags and bunting put out in celebration. Parties were organised in the streets, even pianos rolled out to accompany the singing. Ystradgynlais Brass Band led the dancing that night on the Cross, with Jo Herman's wife Catriona teaching everyone the Highland Fling.

Towards the end of the war Llew decided to retire from teaching and put all his energy into his broadcasting work. In the following fifteen years there was hardly a BBC Wales pamphlet which did not contain examples of his photographs. In the 1952 Eisteddfod at Aberystwyth he was awarded a plaque for winning First Prize in each photography section.

Betty and Howel now settled a few miles down the valley at Pontardawe, where Howel's father, Will Hopkin, was proprietor and editor of *The West Wales Observer*, the local newspaper. Their three daughters benefited greatly from an upbringing divided between the two villages, with both families involved in the arts.

In 1954 Ystradgynlais was chosen as the location for the National Eisteddfod. Llew was invited to join the committee and design the commemorative brochure. For this he sculpted in clay a superb shield and emblem which was adopted as the cover photograph. He judged the Arts and Crafts section, the standard of which had reached professional heights. The week after the Eisteddfod he spent packing and returning the entries to the competitors.

V.E. Day at the White Hart, Llanddarog, Carmarthenshire.

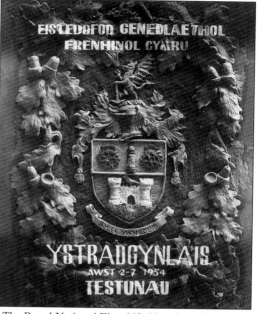

Llew with first granddaughter, Wendy, in his Ynysgedwyn classroom.

The Royal National Eisteddfod brochure. The clay model was designed and made by Llew.

Llew (left) and Walter Bird (third left) judging Eisteddfod competitors.

Sixty years of total commitment to the exacting standards he had set himself was beginning to take its toll. Never having missed a day's work, days which often stretched into the next, Llew now felt his energy begin to wane.

He had made his first television appearance in 1952 in the BBC documentary on the life of Josef Herman, and had not enjoyed the experience. Although gregarious he was far more comfortable out of the limelight, and behind the camera. Nevertheless, he continued to write and illustrate his 'Nature Notes' for *Llais Llafur*, which in a way brought him full circle. For this is where he had started as a young graduate with his 'Diary of a Smallholder' forty years before.

Still excited by the prospect of glimpsing beauty in nature, he passed the art of observation and expression down to his grandchildren, who felt privileged to enjoy these special trips to the mountains or seaside, as their mother had done in the 1920s and 1930s.

In 1959 he was commissioned to prepare seventy drawings, illustrations which were to appear in *Paul a Nesta*, a children's nature book by W. J. Jones. However, the work was very detailed and as soon as he had completed the drawings his health failed him. A few weeks later, on 9 March 1960, he passed away. The book was published by Llyfrau'r Dryw at the end of the year.

Throughout the 1950s Llew had noted, with some sadness, how much village life had changed. There were no longer miners squatting outside the Italian cafe on the Cross. Workers now travelled to the steel works at Margam, or the factories around Swansea. Forests began to cover the scars left by the mining industry, and the new affluence made people, strangely, more insular.

Llew did not live to see the achievements of his grandchildren, nor to know that Mary, the youngest, whom he had encouraged to sing as sweetly as his favourite, Ruby Murray, would become a world success.

Llew with his trusty Rolleiflex camera.

HISTORICAL

Water Street flood, Ystrad, 1916.

Tŷ Coch built by George Crane, owner of the Ynysgedwyn Iron Works in 1840. Taken in 1924.

Hedd Wyn's monument, Trawsfynydd, 1937.

Monument to Llywelyn ap Gruffydd
(The Last Prince), near Cilmeri, 1938.

The congregation arriving on horseback for a service at Soar-y-mynydd, 1930.

A street in Anglesey, August 1928.

Penillion winners at Ammanford National
Eisteddfod, 1922: pupils at Gurnos Primary School.

Sulphur well at Cwm-twrch, near
Ystradgynlais, 1936
(the spring is still in use).

Excavating hut circles on the Beacons, 1932.

Coronation Day of George VI and
Queen Elizabeth, Oddfellow Street,
Ystrad, 1937.

View of Ystradgynlais from Coronation Park showing 'pre-fabs', 1942.

The Drovers' Arms on Mynydd Epynt, 1935.

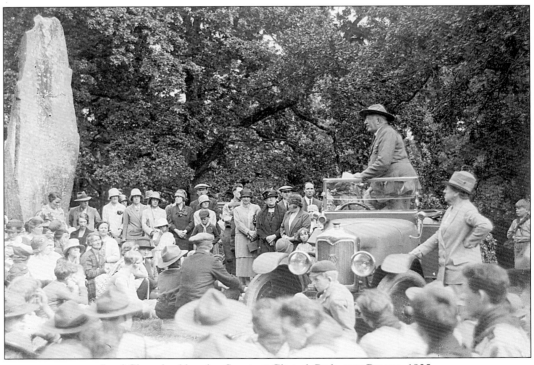

Lord Glanusk addressing Scouts at Glanusk Park, near Brecon, 1935.

At the Wishing Well below
Carreg Cennen castle, 1937.

Caerphilly castle, 1928.

Liverpool evacuees arriving at Ystrad station, 1940.

Cwmgïedd Post Office which featured in the film *The Silent Village*, 1943.

Artist Josef Herman sketching underground at Ynysgedwyn Colliery, 1948.

Colliers leaving Ystalyfera
Colliery, 1957.

The home of
Maurice Hewlett
(1861-1923),
novelist friend of
Llew and Fabian
supporter of the
miners' cause.

At the time of the Colliers' Carnival,
Ystrad, General Strike, 1926.

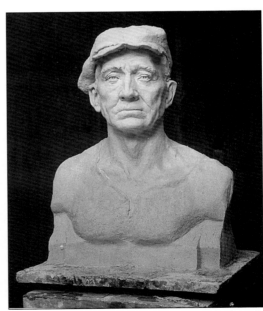

Bust of Dai Grenfell, M.P., who became 'Father of
the House', sculpted by Jenkin Evans R.A., 1940.

Curlew on nest, moorland near Crai, 1938.

Young   cuckoo
being fed, 1920.

Adult   cuckoo,
1918.

A telephoto shot of a peregrine falcon in flight, Abergwesyn, 1935.

Great spotted woodpecker, Rhayader, 1936.

Long-tailed tit, Fairy Glen, Neath valley, 1937.

Mother thrush and young in a garden, Ystrad, 1920. First Prize winner *Weekly Dispatch*.

Young cuckoo and foster parent, on Drum mountain, 1920.

Reynard in his lair, Cwmgïedd, 1938.

Swan, Brynmill Park, Swansea, 1930.

Geese crossing a minor road near Trecastle, 1930.

First love, on an apple tree, Sunny-hill garden, 1920.

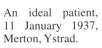

An ideal patient, 11 January 1937, Merton, Ystrad.

'Buddy' on the dunes at Oxwich Bay, Gower, 1934. First Prize, Spillers Competition.

Set of three of Peter, a Welsh springer spaniel, teasing the farm pig, 1930.

Set of four of Peter, the spaniel, asking his friend for milk, 1933.

Bullocks in a field at Tregaron, 1930.

Salmon leaping in the river Usk at Trecastle, 1932.

Two of the best, Brecon farm, 1927. *The "Kodak" Magazine* cover and *Sunday Graphic* First Prize.

Smiths at Cynghordy banding a wheel.

The blacksmith's craft: David Griffiths, Defynnog, making a hoop.

Stacking hay from the slide car, Llanfynydd.

Mechanical rake, Penrock Farm, Pen-y-cae, 1930.

Brickworkers nicknamed 'Lord and Lady Bricks', near Ystradgynlais, 1930.

Cockle women, Llan-saint, Carmarthenshire, 1934.

Fisherman, Ferryside, 1936.

T. Evans, cobbler, Coelbren.

Interior of a
house in the
Tawe valley.

Stocks, Llywel church, near Trecastle, Powys.

Paws of the last
wolf killed in
Wales.
Brecon Museum

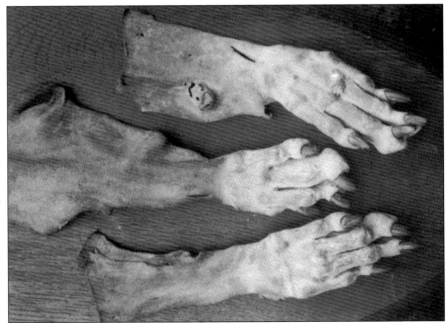

COUNTRYSIDE & TOWNSCAPES

The Lakes, Killarney: Blodwen on left, 1928.

Street scene in Cork, 1928.

Fire on the lower slopes of the Beacons, 1930.

Neath abbey, 1928.

Courtyard at Bere Regis, 1934.

Cottage at Kenfig, near Porthcawl, 1937.

A miner's cottage at Kidwelly. First prize winner in the National Eisteddfod, 1929.

Hiker at cottage, near Dawlish, 1934.

Cottage near
Llangadog,
1928.

A corner of the
old tithe barn,
Willersley
Court,
Winforton,
1928.

Llew with 'Craig' of 'Craig of the Welsh Hills' by Roy Saunders, 1936.

Arch at Worm's Head, Gower, Roy Saunders and 'Craig', 1936.

Valley in mid-Wales, 1938.

Cottage at Kenfig Hill, near Porthcawl, 1937.

View across the Bristol Channel from Rhosili, 1937.

The brow of the hill, Trecastle Road, 1938.

Pitching tent at Crai below Fan Gyhirych, 1937.

Covered gypsy waggons, near Brecon, 1936.

Under the bridge at Ystalyfera, winter 1936.

Blodwen and Betty on the Gower coast, 1925.

Blodwen and
Betty on the
cliff-top opposite
Worm's Head,
Gower, 1926.

On the Drum mountain above Ystrad, 1938.

A shady lane leading to the 'hundred' steps at Pontardawe, 1948.

Storm cloud over the Starvin, Ystrad, 1944.

Wistaria at the Wellington Inn, Newcastle, Gwent, 1946. Published in *Farmer's Weekly*.

View of Caldey Island from the mainland, 1938.

Wind blown trees, Jersey Marine, Swansea, 1938.

Hill-top dwellers: trees on Varteg mountain, 1939. Diffuser used with enlarger to give special effect.

Snow scene on the Swansea-Brecon canal at Ystrad, 1946.

The Holp, Defynnog, 1938.

Swallow Falls, Betws-y-coed, 1940.

Birmingham water-works at Rhayader, 1939.

Glaslyn estuary, 1938.

The Orangery at Margam Abbey, 1947.

The Gateway to Adventure, taken near Rhayader, 1950.

Sgwd yr Henryd, near Coelbren, 1954.

The Menai Bridge, 1952.

Beddgelert. Home of the famous Welsh legend of Prince Llywelyn and his faithful hound, 1952. Published in *The Nation*.

Little mother goose in Sunnyhill field, 1925.

Beauty and the Beast, Salisbury Park, 1922.

Little Red Riding Hood, Sunnyhill, 1922.

Iory and Betty at Langland,
Gower, 1926.

Bathtime, garden at
Sunnyhill, 1925.

'Conkers': garden at Bronwydd, 1928.

Rocking horses, Ynysgedwyn School, 1928.

'Sex Equality', Sunnyhill, 1931.

The Laughing Song: winner of 'Sunripe Cigarettes' competition, 1933.

Kite flying on the Drum mountain, above Ystrad, 1936.

Butterflies at Oxwich Bay, 1937.

Fine weather friends, Sunnyhill: cover for Rowntree's Chocolate box, 1925.

'Not today', Caswell Bay, 1926.

Harvest mice at Rhyl, August 1927. First Prize, *Daily Herald*.

Red sails in the sunset, Poole Harbour, Dorset, 1935.

The joys of cycling: Jane in Bronwydd garden, 1930. First Prize, *Daily Herald*.

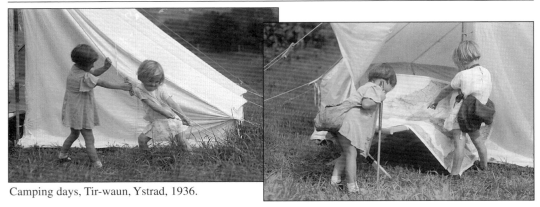

Camping days, Tir-waun, Ystrad, 1936.

Beside the lake, Crai, 1934.

A painting expedition on the Brecon Beacons, 1930.

Young fishergirl, river Tawe at Craig-y-nos, 1937.

Feeding the pigeons, outside St Paul's Cathedral,
London, 1926. Cover of *Snapshots*.

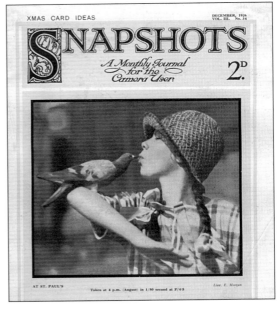

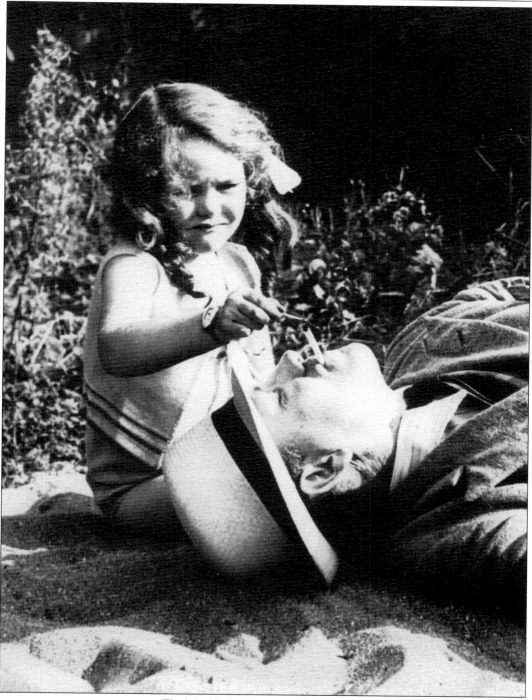

'That's it, Uncle!' Garden at Merton, 1938.

Rovering, Glanusk Park, 1929.

A splashing time, garden at Merton, 1938.

Blodwen and Buddy, Merton, 1940.

Entry for 'Sunripe Cigarettes' competition, 1933.

The Intruder, Merton, 1944.

Making sure it's fresh, Merton, 1944.

'Blue Jeans', Merton, 1944.

'Baby Teeth', Merton, 1944.

'A young snake charmer', Betty and a harmless snake, Devizes, 1922.

Gathering yellow flag iris at Oxwich, 1925.

Blodwen and Betty mushrooming at Devizes, 1922. First Prize, Kodak Magazine.

Seaweed gatherer, Mumbles, 1925.

Homework, Bronwydd, Ystrad, 1928.

Morning gossip at Tintern, 1929. First Prize, *The Schoolmaster* magazine.

Josef Herman, 1947.

A miner's welcome home, Ystrad, 1935.

Dafydd Jacob, octogenarian of the Beacons, 1936.

The Smoker, Bryn-mawr, 1952.

Children of The Strand, Swansea, 1936.

Gypsy boy at Llangadog Common, 1937.

Gypsy girls, outside
Brecon, 1938.

Mother and child,
Llangadog, 1938.

A Christmas party, Swansea Camera Club, 1938.

Cocklewoman, Pen-clawdd, 1938.

A modern hiker, Ystrad, 1934.

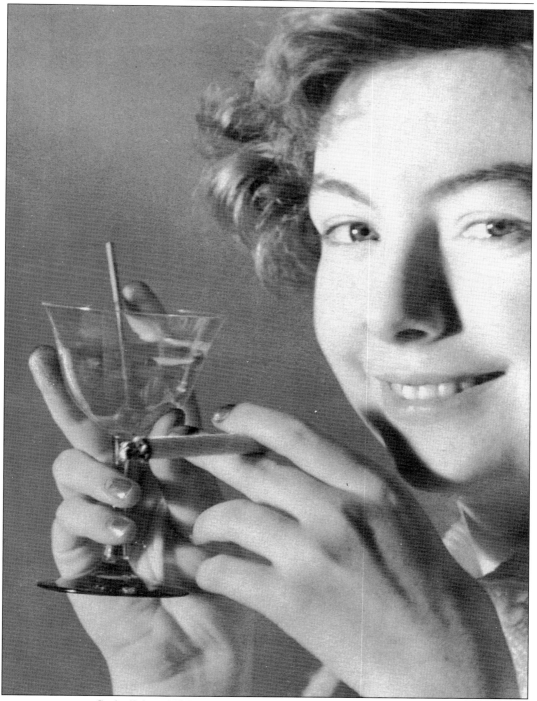

Cocktail time, 1937, at Merton. Prize winner, *The "Kodak" Magazine.*

Night-watchman, The Strand, Swansea, 1935.

The Dreamer, 1954.

News of Dunkirk? Ystrad, 1940.

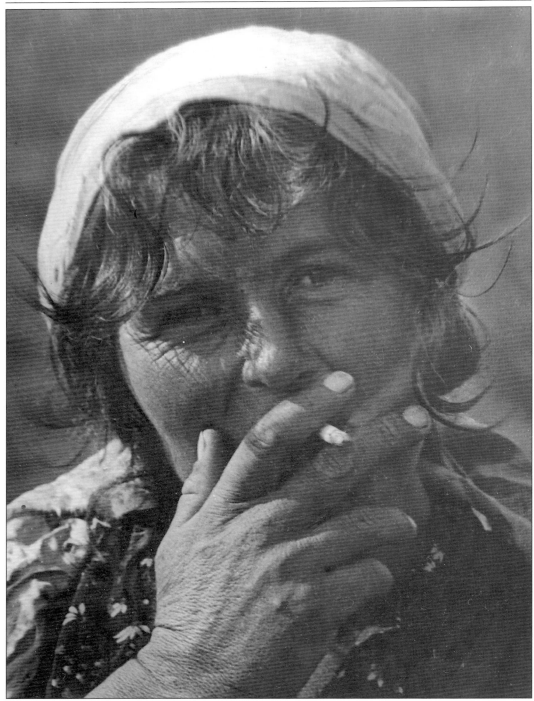

A modern gypsy, 1950.

An idyll, Craig-y-nos, 1945.

Self-portrait, Cwmgïedd, 1935.

APPENDIX

After his first Brownie box camera, Llew bought a Kodak quarter-plate Reflex, but the plate emulsion was slow and the lens had to be stopped down to get a sharp image. This meant a 'long' exposure—quite unsuitable for photographing wildlife. To overcome this he used a silent shutter with the 'click' coming after the picture had been taken, ensuring that the animal would not be startled. Only one or two of the twelve exposures he took of each subject would satisfy his demanding standards.

In the mid 1920s he bought his first Leica, and in 1936 his lifelong favourite—a Rolleiflex. With its magnifier-focusing hood which guaranteed accurate 'fine-focus', and the Zeiss Tessar f3.5 mm lens built into a Compur shutter, working at $\frac{1}{500th}$ of a second, it was perfect for his needs. When he wished to take photographs at meetings, or over the heads of a crowd, he now had the product to do the job, with its 'finder' lens on top and its 'taking' lens below.

It was also in the 1930s that Panchromatic plates were produced. These were sensitive to all colours, unlike the Orthochromatic plates (where red objects would appear black) that Llew had been using previously.

In 1935 G.E.C. had brought out the first Saschlite bulbs, which were filled with crumpled aluminium foil in oxygen. These gave a flash which lasted $\frac{1}{50th}$ of a second. Five years later, in 1940, Dawe Instruments brought out the first portable electronic 'flash' units which gave an exposure of $\frac{1}{5000th}$ of a second and 'stopped' birds in full flight.

Llew's technical improvements were often due to his own efforts and experiments. Money was usually a problem, and when in 1934 he felt extremely frustrated by the cost of the new glazing machines, he decided to perfect his own method. He bought half a dozen chromium-plated sheets, each taking two 10" x 8" prints. The wet prints were laid face down on the immaculately cleaned chrome, and the excess moisture pressed out with a roller. The plates, with the adhering prints, were then wrapped so tightly in linen cloth that they curved into an arc. These were then placed in front of the fire to dry for about twenty minutes. When the tapes were untied, the prints fell off to reveal a brilliant professional sheen. Not one to keep his secrets to himself, Llew wrote to *The "Kodak" Magazine* who commissioned him to write an article on the process.

By the 1940s, with a little more income but certainly less free time, Llew invested in a glazing machine. Its immense bulk became a permanent feature in Merton's bathroom.